Digital Defenders: A Gu..

"Digital Defenders" is book that is intended be utilized as a starting point to engage and equip your young readers to become responsible digital citizens. With the amount of information accessed on the internet, empower your young digital surfers with the knowledge and tools to protect themselves and others in this digital world.

Contents

Preface 3
Psychological effects of Cyberbullying by age group 9
    Age Group 6-10: 9
    Age Group 11-13: 10
    Age Group 14-17: 10
Age Group 6-10 11
"My Online Adventure: Exploring the Digital World Safely" 11
    Chapter 1: "What is the Internet?" 11
    Chapter 2: "Safe Surfing: Navigating Age-Appropriate Websites" 12
    Chapter 3: "Cybersecurity Basics: Safeguarding Your Digital Castle" 13
    Chapter 4: "Being a Cyberbullying Buster: Spreading Kindness in the Digital Kingdom" 14
    Chapter 5: "Kindness Counts: Spreading Positivity in the Digital Kingdom" 16
    Chapter 6: "Becoming a Digital Hero: Protecting the Digital Kingdom" 17
Age Group 11-13 19
"The Digital Pathfinders: Navigating the Online Maze Responsibly" 19
    Chapter 1: Cybersecurity Fundamentals 19
        Building Strong Passwords 19
        Recognizing Phishing Attempts 19
        Protecting Against Online Threats 20
    Chapter 2: Ethical Digital Citizenship 20
        Understanding Your Digital Footprint 20
        The Power of Responsible Behavior 21
        Contributing Positively 21

Chapter 3: Social Media Smarts 21
- Navigating Social Media Responsibly 21
- Setting Privacy Settings 22
- Avoiding Oversharing 22

Chapter 3: Cyberbullying Prevention 22
- Recognizing Cyberbullying 23
- Strategies to Prevent Cyberbullying 23
- Reporting and Seeking Help 23
- Cultivating Digital Empathy 23

Chapter 5: Online Relationships & avoiding Catfishing. 24
- The World of Online Friendships 24
- Safeguarding Your Boundaries 24
- Navigating Tricky Situations 24
- The Quest for Authenticity 24
- Handling Online Conflict 25
- The Value of Offline Connections 25

Chapter 5: Becoming a Cyber Defender 25
- Critical Thinking Online 25
- Evaluating Online Information 26
- Staying Safe on the Internet 26
- Embracing Lifelong Learning 26
- Leading by Example 26
- Making a Difference 27
- The Journey Continues 27

Chapter 6: Cybersecurity Fundamentals 27

Age Group 14-17 27

"Guardians of the Digital Realm: Empowering Responsible Online Citizenship" 27

Chapter 1: Digital Footprint and Reputation Management 28
- Understanding Your Digital Footprint 28
- Maintaining a Positive Digital Identity 28

Chapter 2: Social Media Influence 29
- Recognizing Social Media's Impact 29
- Developing Healthy Online Habits 29

Digital Respect: Protecting your Online Persona	30
Chapter 3: Cyber Ethics	31
Exploring Cyber Ethics	31
Respecting Others' Rights Online	31
Chapter 4: Cyberbullying Intervention	32
Taking Action Against Cyberbullying	32
Supporting Others	33
Chapter 5: Cybersecurity Careers	33
Exploring Careers in Cybersecurity	33
The Importance of Skilled Professionals	34
Chapter 6: Advanced Cybersecurity	34
The Power of Encryption	35
Navigating Secure Wi-Fi Usage	35
Protecting Personal Data	35

Preface

Parents/guardians,

If you are reading this, you as much as I, are concerned about the digital age and protecting our children from what we don't want them to see, and how this effects the mental health of your children. This book is for you as much as it is for your young readers as a starting point to encourage communication between you and your young readers.

In the rapidly evolving digital landscape, the importance of cybersecurity, cyberbullying prevention, and responsible social media use cannot be overstated. "Digital Defenders" is a comprehensive guide tailored to different age groups, from 6 to 17 years old. This book aims to equip young readers with the knowledge and skills they need to navigate the online world safely, responsibly, and confidently.

Chapter 1: Age Group 6-10 Title: "My Online Adventure: Exploring the Digital World Safely"

- Introduction to the Internet: Understanding what the internet is and how it works.
- Safe Surfing: Learning how to explore age-appropriate websites and avoiding harmful content.
- Cybersecurity Basics: Introduction to online password safety, keeping personal information private, and seeking help from trusted adults.
- Cyberbullying Awareness: Recognizing cyberbullying and what to do if they encounter it.

- Kindness Counts: Emphasizing the importance of treating others online with respect and empathy.
- Becoming a Digital Hero: Understanding how to protect themselves and their friends from online risks, becoming digital hero's.

Chapter 2: Age Group 11-13 Title: "The Digital Pathfinders: Navigating the Online Maze Responsibly"

- Cyber safety Fundamentals: Building strong passwords, recognizing phishing attempts, and protecting against online threats.
- Ethical Digital Citizenship: Understanding the impact of online behavior and how it contributes positively to the digital community.
- Social Media Smarts: Navigating social media responsibly, setting privacy settings, and avoiding oversharing.
- Cyberbullying Prevention: Recognizing the signs of cyberbullying and strategies to prevent and report it.
- Online Relationships: Understanding the risks and challenges of forming connections with others online.
- Becoming a Cyber Defender: Developing critical thinking skills to evaluate online information and staying safe on the internet.

Chapter 3: Age Group 14-17 Title: "Guardians of the Digital Realm: Empowering Responsible Online Citizenship"

- Digital Footprint and Reputation Management: Understanding the long-term implications of online actions and how they contribute to maintaining a positive digital identity.
- Cyber Ethics: Exploring the ethical considerations of technology use and respecting others' rights online.
- Social Media Influence: Recognizing the impact of social media on mental health and developing healthy online habits.
- Cyberbullying Intervention: Taking action against cyberbullying and supporting others who may be affected.
- Advanced Cybersecurity: Learning about encryption, secure Wi-Fi usage, and protecting personal data.
- Cybersecurity Careers: Exploring various careers in cybersecurity and the importance of skilled professionals in safeguarding the digital world.

Teaching all age groups, the importance of cyber security, cyberbullying prevention, and responsible navigation of social media is crucial in today's digital age for several reasons:

1. Online Safety: Understanding cyber security helps children protect their personal information, devices, and online accounts from hackers and cybercriminals. Teaching them to use strong passwords and avoid sharing sensitive data helps reduce the risk of identity theft and other online threats.
2. Protection from Cyberbullying: Educating children about cyberbullying and its consequences empowers them to recognize and address such behavior. Knowing how to respond to cyberbullying and where to seek help can protect them and others from emotional harm.
3. Digital Footprint Awareness: Teaching children about their digital footprint instills an understanding that their online actions leave a trace. Encouraging responsible social media use helps shape a positive online reputation, which can impact future educational and career opportunities.
4. Critical Thinking: Learning how to navigate social media responsibly involves developing critical thinking skills. Children need to discern reliable information, recognize online manipulation, and evaluate the credibility of sources they encounter on the internet.
5. Empowering Digital Citizenship: Understanding cyber security and responsible online behavior fosters the development of responsible digital citizenship. Children learn to respect others' privacy, interact kindly online, and contribute positively to online communities.
6. Protection from Online Scams: Knowledge of cyber security enables children to recognize phishing attempts and other online scams. This helps them avoid falling victim to deceptive tactics and protects them from potential financial losses.
7. Safer Online Relationships: Learning about the risks and challenges of online relationships helps children develop healthier online connections. They can differentiate between genuine friendships and potential risks posed by strangers on the internet.
8. Mental Health Awareness: Understanding the influence of social media and its potential impact on mental health encourages children to use social media in moderation and maintain a balanced online-offline lifestyle.
9. Ethical Digital Behavior: Teaching children the ethics of online behavior encourages them to act responsibly, avoid cyberbullying, and refrain from engaging in harmful or illegal activities on the internet.
10. Parent-Child Communication: Educating children about cyber security and responsible online practices opens channels for meaningful parent-child conversations. It allows parents to stay informed about their children's online experiences and provide appropriate guidance and support.

Overall, teaching cyber security, cyberbullying prevention, and responsible social media use is essential for equipping children of all ages with the necessary knowledge and skills to navigate the digital world safely and responsibly. By instilling these principles early on, we can foster a generation of responsible digital citizens who use technology for positive purposes while safeguarding their own and others' well-being online.

Teaching 6 to 10-year-olds about cyber security, cyberbullying, and navigating social media requires a delicate and age-appropriate approach. Here are some strategies to effectively convey these concepts to young children:

1. Interactive Storytelling: Use engaging and relatable stories to illustrate the importance of cybersecurity, cyberbullying prevention, and safe social media use. Create characters they can identify with, facing online challenges and making responsible decisions.

2. Role-Playing Games: Organize role-playing games where children can act out different online scenarios, teaching them how to respond to cyberbullying, suspicious messages, or requests for personal information.

3. Use Child-Friendly Language: Explain cybersecurity concepts in simple terms using language that kids can understand. Avoid technical jargon and make the information relatable to their daily lives.

4. Establish Trust: Create a safe and open environment where children feel comfortable sharing their online experiences, questions, and concerns. Encourage them to talk about any cyberbullying incidents they witness or experience.

5. Cybersecurity Superheroes: Introduce the idea of "cybersecurity superheroes" who protect their online world. Teach them that they can be responsible digital citizens by using strong passwords, protecting personal information, and being kind to others online.

6. Privacy and Personal Information: Explain the importance of keeping personal information private and not sharing it with strangers online. Teach them what information is safe to share and what should remain confidential.

7. Cyberbullying Awareness: Define cyberbullying and help them understand the impact it can have on others. Encourage empathy and kindness while emphasizing the need to report any instances of cyberbullying.

8. Safe Social Media Usage: If they use social media platforms designed for kids under parental supervision, teach them about safe practices, the importance of setting privacy settings, and how to report inappropriate content or users.

9. Recognizing Suspicious Messages: Teach children how to identify suspicious messages or requests and emphasize the importance of not clicking on unknown links or downloading files from strangers.

10. Parental Involvement: Involve parents or guardians in the educational process by sharing information about what their children are learning and encouraging them to reinforce these lessons at home.

11. Limit Screen Time: Promote healthy screen time habits and emphasize the importance of balancing online activities with physical and social activities offline.

12. Rewards for Responsible Behavior: Recognize and reward responsible online behavior, such as reporting cyberbullying or following safe social media practices.

13. Online Safety Pledges: Encourage children to create their online safety pledges, committing to be responsible digital citizens and promoting positive online behavior.

Remember, at this age, children are still developing their understanding of the online world, and reinforcement is vital. Keep the lessons positive, engaging, and relevant to their lives to ensure that they absorb and apply these important lessons about cybersecurity and responsible digital behavior.

Teaching 11 to 13-year-olds about cyber security, cyberbullying, and navigating social media demands a more comprehensive and nuanced approach, as they are entering their teenage years and may be more active online. Here are some effective strategies to educate them about these important topics:

1. Open Discussions: Initiate open discussions about their online experiences, the apps, and platforms they use, and any concerns they may have. Create a safe and non-judgmental space for them to share their experiences and ask questions.

2. Real-Life Examples: Use age-appropriate real-life examples of cyberbullying incidents, privacy breaches, and online scams to demonstrate the real-world consequences of unsafe online behavior.

3. Privacy and Social Media: Teach them about the importance of privacy settings on social media platforms and how to control who can see their posts and personal information. It's worth mentioning that they should be cautious about sharing location information and avoid posting any details that reveal their exact location.

4. Online Persona: Discuss the concept of an online persona and how it can differ from their real-life self. Teach them to be mindful of what they share online and how it can impact their reputation.

5. Cyberbullying Awareness: Define cyberbullying and provide practical tips on how to respond to and prevent cyberbullying. Encourage empathy and the importance of reporting such incidents.

6. Digital Footprint: Explain the concept of a digital footprint and how their online actions can leave a lasting impact. Emphasize the need to maintain a positive digital reputation.

7. Recognizing Phishing: Teach them how to recognize phishing attempts and suspicious messages. Show them how to verify the authenticity of emails and websites before sharing personal information.

8. Password Security: Reinforce the importance of using strong, unique passwords for each online account and introduce the idea of using password managers.

9. Online Friendships: Discuss the risks of making friends with strangers online and the importance of only connecting with people they know in real life.

10. Social Media Peer Pressure: Address the issue of peer pressure on social media and teach them how to say "no" to sharing or participating in harmful or inappropriate content.

11. Secure Wi-Fi Usage: Explain the risks of using public Wi-Fi networks and encourage them to connect to secure and trusted networks.

12. Reporting Mechanisms: Inform them about reporting mechanisms on social media platforms and other online services. Show them how to report inappropriate content, cyberbullying, or suspicious behavior.

13. Encourage Critical Thinking: Teach them to think critically about the information they encounter online and to verify facts before sharing or believing in something they read or see.

14. Balancing Screen Time: Discuss the importance of balancing online activities with offline activities, including hobbies, physical exercise, and spending time with family and friends.

15. Real-World Consequences: Help them understand that their online actions can have real-world consequences, both positive and negative, and emphasize the need for responsible online behavior. You can add a specific example of a positive real-world consequence, such as a teenager using their online presence to raise awareness for a charitable cause.

16. Empower Them to Seek Help: Let them know they can always seek help from a trusted adult if they encounter any concerning or uncomfortable situations online.

It's essential to approach these topics with sensitivity and age-appropriate language. Encourage them to be responsible digital citizens and empower them to make safe and informed choices while navigating the online world.

Teaching 14 to 17-year-olds about cyber security, cyberbullying, and navigating social media requires an approach that acknowledges their increased independence and online presence. Here are some effective strategies to educate them about these critical topics:

1. Interactive Workshops: Find interactive workshops or classes that engage teenagers in hands-on activities related to cyber security, importance of creating strong passwords, identifying phishing emails, and understanding encryption.

2. Case Studies: Use real-world case studies of cyber-attacks, data breaches, and cyberbullying incidents to illustrate the real consequences of online threats and the importance of cybersecurity.

3. Privacy and Social Media: Discuss the intricacies of privacy settings on social media platforms and the potential risks associated with oversharing personal information.

4. Ethical Hacking: Introduce ethical hacking concepts and explain how ethical hackers play a crucial role in identifying and fixing security vulnerabilities.

5. Cyber Ethics: Engage in discussions about cyber ethics and the responsible use of technology, addressing issues like online harassment and digital citizenship.

6. Online Reputation Management: Highlight the importance of maintaining a positive online reputation and how online behavior can impact future opportunities. Also, consider highlighting the importance of critical thinking when evaluating information online, especially in the context of personal branding.

7. Digital Footprint and Personal Branding: Teach them about the concept of a digital footprint and how to curate a positive and authentic online presence that aligns with their values and goals.
8. Social Media Influences: Discuss the influence of social media on self-esteem, body image, and mental health. Encourage them to recognize and counteract negative influences.
9. Cyberbullying Prevention: Provide practical strategies to prevent and address cyberbullying, such as reporting incidents and supporting friends who may be targeted.
10. Online Relationships: Discuss the risks and challenges of online relationships, including the importance of being cautious when interacting with strangers on the internet.
11. Social Engineering Awareness: Educate them about social engineering tactics used by cybercriminals and how to avoid falling victim to scams and manipulation.
12. Safe Online Shopping: Teach them about secure online shopping practices, including using reputable websites and payment methods, and avoiding fake online stores.
13. Ethical Use of Technology: Emphasize the importance of using technology responsibly and avoiding engaging in harmful or illegal activities online.
14. Parental Communication: Encourage open communication between teenagers and their parents or guardians about their online experiences, concerns, and questions.
15. Practical Cybersecurity Exercises: Engage them in practical cybersecurity exercises, such as conducting security assessments on their own devices or creating secure online accounts.

By approaching these topics with relevance to their lives and fostering open discussions, teenagers can become informed and responsible digital citizens who can navigate the online world safely and ethically.

By understanding the significance of cybersecurity, cyberbullying prevention, and navigating social media responsibly, they can confidently embark on their digital journeys while contributing to a safer and more positive digital community. Remember, the digital realm holds countless opportunities, but with great power comes great responsibility.

Psychological effects of Cyberbullying by age group

The psychological effects of cyberbullying can vary depending on the age group of the individuals involved. Here are the general psychological effects observed in age groups 6-10, 11-14, and 15-17:

Age Group 6-10:

1. Anxiety and Fear: Young children in this age group may experience heightened anxiety and fear due to the online harassment they face. They might become scared of using the internet or digital devices altogether.
2. Low Self-Esteem: Cyberbullying can negatively impact a child's self-esteem and self-worth. They may feel inadequate and develop a negative self-image as a result of hurtful online comments or messages.

3. Social Withdrawal: Cyberbullying can lead to social withdrawal as children may avoid social interactions, both online and offline, to protect themselves from further harm.
4. Academic Problems: The psychological stress caused by cyberbullying can interfere with a child's ability to concentrate and perform well in school.
5. Physical Symptoms: Some children may experience physical symptoms such as headaches, stomachaches, or trouble sleeping due to the emotional distress caused by cyberbullying.

Age Group 11-13:
1. Depression: Cyberbullying can trigger feelings of sadness, hopelessness, and worthlessness, leading to symptoms of depression in this age group.
2. Increased Stress: Adolescents in this age group may experience heightened stress levels as a result of cyberbullying, affecting their overall well-being.
3. School Avoidance: Cyberbullying may lead to school avoidance and a decline in academic performance as victims may try to escape the bullying environment.
4. Social Isolation: Victims of cyberbullying might withdraw from social activities, both online and offline, and have difficulty forming trusting relationships.
5. Emotional Instability: Adolescents may exhibit emotional volatility, experiencing mood swings and irritability due to the ongoing cyberbullying trauma.

Age Group 14-17:
1. Anxiety Disorders: Cyberbullying can contribute to the development of anxiety disorders in older teens, leading to persistent feelings of worry and apprehension.
2. Suicidal Thoughts: The emotional toll of cyberbullying can be severe, and in some cases, it may lead to suicidal thoughts or self-harm behaviors.
3. Academic Decline: The psychological impact of cyberbullying can lead to a decline in academic performance, further exacerbating feelings of inadequacy.
4. Substance Abuse: Some teenagers may turn to substances as a coping mechanism to deal with the stress and emotional pain caused by cyberbullying.
5. Dissociation: Victims of cyberbullying may emotionally dissociate from the online world or try to dissociate from their emotions as a coping mechanism.

It is essential for parents, educators, and caregivers to be vigilant about cyberbullying and its potential effects on children and teenagers. Early intervention, open communication, and providing a supportive environment are crucial in helping victims cope with cyberbullying and promoting responsible online behavior.

Age Group 6-10

"My Online Adventure: Exploring the Digital World Safely"

Chapter 1: "What is the Internet?"

Once upon a time in a digital world, there was a magical place called the Internet. It was like a vast treasure trove filled with information, fun, and exciting adventures. Let's join our curious young explorers, Alex and Maya, as they embark on a journey to understand what the Internet is and how it works.

Alex and Maya were eager to learn about this magical place, so they asked their tech-savvy friend, Teacher tech, to guide them. Teacher tech was known for his knowledge of all things digital and was thrilled to be their guide.

"Welcome, young adventurers!" Teacher tech said with a smile. "The Internet is like a massive library that contains books, pictures, music, and videos. But instead of shelves and books, it uses invisible pathways called 'websites' to store all this information. These websites are like rooms filled with fascinating things to explore."

As they walked through the virtual halls of the Internet, Alex asked, "But how do we access these websites, Teacher tech?"

"Ah, that's the magic of it all!" replied Teacher tech. "We use devices like computers, tablets, or smartphones, which connect to the Internet. Once we're connected, we can type the address of a website into a search bar, and voilà! The website appears on our screens."

Maya was amazed by the colorful websites they visited, each offering something unique and exciting. "But Teacher tech, how does the information travel from one place to another?"

Teacher tech grinned. "That's the best part! The information travels through folders called 'data packets,' which are like little files carrying the information from one place to another. They zip through the invisible pathways of the Internet, making sure you get what you want in a blink of an eye!"

Alex and Maya were fascinated by the explanation, but they also questioned if everything on the Internet was safe. "Teacher tech, how can we make sure we're safe while exploring this magical place?" asked Alex.

"Ah, you're right to be cautious," replied Teacher tech. "Just like in the real world, there are some places in the digital world that may not be safe for young adventurers like you. That's why we have to practice safe surfing."

"Safe surfing? What's that?" Maya asked curiously.

Teacher tech smiled. "Safe surfing means exploring age-appropriate websites and avoiding hurtful content. You should never share personal information like your full name, address, phone number or pictures with strangers online. And remember, if you come across something that makes you uncomfortable or scared, always tell a trusted adult about it."

Armed with this knowledge, Alex and Maya felt more confident and prepared to continue their Internet adventure. They thanked Teacher tech for being such a fantastic guide and promised to use their newfound knowledge responsibly.

As they ventured further into the digital world, Alex and Maya knew they were on the right path to become smart Internet explorers. The Internet had become an exciting place of knowledge and fun, and they were ready to embrace the magic while always staying safe.

And so, their Internet adventure had just begun, filled with endless possibilities and opportunities to learn and grow. With Teacher tech's wisdom and their curiosity, Alex and Maya were ready to explore the vast wonders of the digital world, one website at a time.

Chapter 2: "Safe Surfing: Navigating Age-Appropriate Websites"

As Alex and Maya continued their Internet adventure, they stumbled upon a sparkling virtual ocean filled with countless websites. Each website seemed to hold a new treasure waiting to be explored. But before they dove in, Teacher tech reminded them about the importance of safe surfing.

"Ah, safe surfing is like exploring a magical sea," Teacher tech said, "where some places are like safe islands, while others may have hidden dangers."

Curious and eager to learn, Alex asked, "How do we know which websites are safe, Teacher tech?"

Teacher tech replied, "To be safe surfers, we need to use our trusty compass called 'common sense.' Look for websites that are recommended for your age group, like educational sites, fun games, and activities that you enjoy. You can also ask your parents, teachers, or other trusted adults for suggestions."

Maya added, "What about websites that might not be safe for us?"

"Great question, Maya!" said Teacher tech. "Websites that ask for personal information, show scary or angry content, or make you feel uncomfortable are like giant sharks. If you encounter any of these, remember to steer away immediately and tell a trusted adult about it."

Teacher tech then showed them how to spot a safe website by looking for a small padlock symbol in the web address bar. "The padlock means the website uses a special shield called 'encryption,' which helps keep your information safe from prying eyes," he explained.

Eager to put their knowledge to the test, Alex and Maya used their compass of common sense to explore age-appropriate websites. They found a treasure trove of educational games, interactive stories, and fun quizzes that captured their interest. There will be times where trusted websites or Apps will question you, to ensure you are of the appropriate age to access games or websites, always ask an adult for help before you enter.

As they ventured deeper into the Internet ocean, they encountered a website that seemed suspicious. The website promised them a chance to win a fabulous prize, but something felt off. Remembering what Teacher tech said, they quickly turned away from the tempting offer and reported it to their parents.

"Well done, my young adventurers!" Teacher tech praised them. "You just demonstrated safe surfing in action. It's essential to avoid websites that promise too-good-to-be-true prizes or ask for personal information. Trust your instincts and always seek help from trusted adults if you're unsure."

Feeling empowered, Alex and Maya continued their exploration with newfound confidence. They navigated the virtual ocean, riding the waves of safe websites and avoiding the hidden dangers of unsafe ones. Each website they visited held exciting knowledge and fun adventures, proving that safe surfing could be both educational and enjoyable.

As the sun set on their Internet adventure for the day, Alex and Maya reflected on what they had learned. They now knew that just like in the real world, exploring the digital world required mindfulness and caution. Armed with their compass of common sense, they were ready to continue their safe surfing journey, always remembering to stay vigilant and protect themselves from any rough waters that might come their way.

And so, their safe surfing exploration had only just begun, and with each website they visited, Alex and Maya knew they were becoming more comfortable at navigating the vast and magical sea of the Internet. They were now true Digital Heroes, ready to venture further into the digital realm with confidence, curiosity, and safety as their guiding stars.

Chapter 3: "Cybersecurity Basics: Safeguarding Your Digital Castle"

With their compass of common sense and newfound knowledge of safe surfing, Alex and Maya continued their digital adventure, feeling more confident in the vast online world. As they sailed further into the virtual sea, they encountered a towering castle guarded by a brave knight named Sir Firewall.

"Ahoy, young adventurers!" greeted Sir Firewall. "I am the protector of this digital castle, and my duty is to keep it safe from any intruders or mischief-makers. Welcome to the realm of cybersecurity basics!"

Curious to learn more, Alex and Maya eagerly listened to Sir Firewall's wisdom.

"Cybersecurity is like building strong walls around your digital castle," explained Sir Firewall. "Just like you lock your home to keep it safe, you must protect your digital world too."

"Can you show us how, Sir Firewall?" asked Maya.

"Of course! One of the most crucial things in cybersecurity is creating strong passwords," said Sir Firewall. "A strong password is like a sturdy gate that keeps intruders out. Make sure your passwords are long, unique, and a mix of letters, numbers, and special characters. Do not use your name or birthday and never share your passwords with anyone, not even your best friend!"

Alex nodded and asked, "What else can we do to protect our digital castle?"

Sir Firewall replied, "Another essential tool is the magic shield called 'antivirus.' It helps defend your digital castle from nasty viruses that might try to sneak in and make your device sick."

"And what about personal information?" Maya inquired.

Sir Firewall smiled, "Ah, personal information is like treasure, and you must keep it safe from prying eyes. Be cautious about what you share online. Never give your full name, address, phone number, pictures, or any personal details to strangers. If someone asks for such information, report it to a parent or trusted adult."

As they explored the digital castle, Alex spotted a magic book lying on a table. "What's that book, Sir Firewall?"

"That, young explorer, is the Book of Digital Updates," replied Sir Firewall. "Just like your castle needs maintenance, your devices and software require regular updates. These updates are like magic potions that fix bugs and protect your digital world from new threats."

Alex and Maya realized that cybersecurity was not just about building walls but also staying vigilant and proactive in protecting their digital castle.

"Now," said Sir Firewall, "I have one last tip for you. If you ever encounter a cyberbully or someone behaving unkindly online, don't fight them alone. Reach out to your digital kingdom's wise advisors, like your parents, teachers, or school counselors, who can offer guidance and support."

As they bid farewell to Sir Firewall, Alex and Maya felt like true knights armed with the knowledge to safeguard their digital castle. They knew that protecting their online world was as important as protecting their physical world.

And so, their journey continued with a new understanding of cybersecurity basics. As they ventured into the vast digital realm, Alex and Maya knew they were well-prepared to defend their castle from any digital dragons that might come their way. With strong passwords, antivirus shields, and a vigilant watch, they were the digital knights of their digital kingdom, ready to explore and learn safely in the magical land of the Internet.

Chapter 4: "Being a Cyberbullying Buster: Spreading Kindness in the Digital Kingdom"

As Alex and Maya continued their digital adventure, they were determined to make the virtual world a kind and welcoming place for everyone they encountered. With their compass of common sense and newfound knowledge of cybersecurity, they set out on a quest to become Cyberbullying Busters.

Along their journey, they met a wise owl named Wise Feather, who was known for his wisdom and kindness. Wise Feather explained that cyberbullying was like a dark cloud that could cast a shadow on the digital kingdom.

"My young Cyberbullying Busters," said Wise Feather, "cyberbullying is when someone uses their digital powers to hurt, scare, or be unkind to others online. It can happen through mean comments, spreading rumors, or sharing hurtful images or sharing embarrassing photos of someone without their knowledge or permission."

Alex and Maya nodded, eager to learn how they could make a difference.

"To be a Cyberbullying Buster, you must be like rays of sunshine that brighten the digital world," Wise Feather continued. "Spread kindness, empathy, and respect in everything you do online."

The duo realized that even small acts of kindness could have a big impact on someone's day. They decided to befriend everyone they met, supporting others when they needed it and reporting any acts of cyberbullying they witnessed.

As they ventured further into the digital kingdom, they encountered a virtual village filled with different characters from all walks of life. They saw a group of friendly avatars engaged in a game, cheering each other on. It was a heartwarming sight, and Alex and Maya knew they had the power to foster this positive environment.

"Let's be like these avatars and show kindness to everyone we meet," Maya suggested.

"You're right," Alex agreed. "We can start by sending kind messages to those who might be feeling down or left out."

They set out on their mission, sending thoughtful messages and uplifting comments to their digital friends. The impact was magical, as they saw smiles and appreciation blossom across the virtual village.

But as they explored further, they encountered a dark corner of the digital kingdom, where an avatar named Alex123 was being targeted by mean comments.

"We can't let this happen," said Maya, her heart filled with compassion.

They stood together, and encouraged other avatars to stand with them demonstrating the power of unity against cyberbullying. They reported the hurtful comments to their parents and reached out to support Alex123.

"Thank you for standing up for me," said Alex123. "I was feeling so alone, but now I know I have friends who care."

Alex and Maya felt proud of their bravery, knowing that they had made a difference in someone's life.

As their quest continued, they encountered more cyberbullying situations. Each time, they stepped forward to be Cyberbullying Busters, spreading kindness and reporting any unkind behavior.

Wise Feather watched with pride as the young Cyberbullying Busters made the digital kingdom a better place. "Remember, my brave ones," he said, "your acts of kindness create ripples of positivity that touch the hearts of others. You have the power to change the digital world for the better."

Filled with gratitude, Alex and Maya continued their journey as Cyberbullying Busters, knowing that their compassion and empathy were the magic keys to unlock a world of kindness in the digital kingdom.

And so, their adventure continued with a newfound purpose. Armed with kindness and courage, they were ready to stand up against cyberbullying and be the shining beacons of light in the vast and magical realm of the Internet.

Chapter 5: "Kindness Counts: Spreading Positivity in the Digital Kingdom"

As Alex and Maya continued their digital adventure, they realized that the power of kindness was not limited to combating cyberbullying; it could also create a ripple effect of positivity in the digital kingdom. With Wise Feather's guidance, they set out on a quest to make the Internet a place where kindness reigned supreme.

They wandered through a virtual forest, where they encountered different avatars, each with unique interests and talents. Alex and Maya learned that every avatar had a story, and behind every screen was a real person with feelings, dreams, and hopes.

"We must treat others with kindness and empathy," Maya said, her heart touched by the diversity of the digital kingdom.

"Absolutely," Alex agreed. "Everyone deserves respect and a chance to shine."

They decided to be the supporter of kindness and to celebrate the uniqueness of each avatar they met. They left friendly comments on artwork, complimented avatars' achievements, and encouraged others to pursue their passions.

In one corner of the virtual forest, they found a virtual school where avatars attended classes to learn and grow. But they also noticed an avatar named TimidTom, who seemed hesitant to participate.

"We should help TimidTom feel welcome and included," suggested Alex.

Maya agreed, and together, they approached TimidTom with warm smiles and open hearts. They introduced themselves and offered to be friends. Gradually, TimidTom's confidence grew, and soon, he was actively engaging with others in the virtual classroom.

Their acts of kindness didn't go unnoticed. Other avatars in the virtual school were inspired by Alex and Maya's actions and started being kinder to one another too. The virtual classroom transformed into a supportive and nurturing environment, where everyone felt valued and heard.

As they ventured further into the digital kingdom, they discovered an online community centered around creativity and storytelling. They encountered an avatar named ArtisticAnnie, who shared her beautiful artwork with the world. Alex and Maya were awestruck by her talent.

"We should let ArtisticAnnie know how amazing her art is," said Maya.

They sent ArtisticAnnie a heartfelt message, praising her talent and dedication. To their delight, ArtisticAnnie responded with gratitude and a willingness to collaborate on a creative project together. Their friendship blossomed, and they found joy in inspiring each other's artistic endeavors.

Throughout their journey, Alex and Maya saw how even the simplest acts of kindness could make a significant impact. They realized that in the digital kingdom, just as in the real world, kindness had the power to brighten someone's day, foster connections, and create a community of support.

As they approached the end of their adventure, they reflected on the lessons they had learned. "Being kind is like spreading magic wherever we go," Alex said.

"And the best part is, we can be kind not just in the digital world but in the real world too," added Maya.

Wise Feather, who had been observing their journey, approached them with a smile. "You have both become true ambassadors of kindness," he said. "Remember that even the smallest act of kindness can create a chain reaction of positivity."

As they bid farewell to Wise Feather, Alex and Maya felt a sense of fulfillment. They knew that the lessons they had learned during their digital adventure would stay with them forever. They had not only become savvy explorers of the digital kingdom but also champions of kindness, ready to create a world where empathy, respect, and positivity reigned supreme.

And so, their adventure may have ended, but the magic of kindness they had sown in the digital kingdom would continue to flourish, spreading its light to every corner of the digital realm and beyond. With hearts full of compassion and spirits full of kindness, Alex and Maya knew they were ready to embark on new adventures, both in the digital world and in the world around them, always remembering that kindness counts, no matter where they went.

Chapter 6: "Becoming a Digital Hero: Protecting the Digital Kingdom"

As Alex and Maya's digital adventure drew to a close, they knew that their journey had transformed them into brave and responsible young digital citizens. They had learned about safe surfing, cybersecurity, cyberbullying prevention, and the power of spreading kindness. Now, they were ready to take their final step in becoming true Digital Heroes.

Wise Feather appeared before them one last time, his eyes gleaming with pride. "Congratulations, my young adventurers," he said. "You have shown great courage, wisdom, and kindness throughout your journey. Now, it is time for you to become true Digital Heroes and protect the digital kingdom from any lurking threats."

Alex and Maya felt a surge of excitement and determination. They understood that being Digital Heroes came with great responsibility, and they were ready to embrace it wholeheartedly.

"To be Digital Heroes, you must always remember the three pillars of digital citizenship: Be safe, be responsible, and be kind," Wise Feather explained. "As you explore the digital world, keep these principles close to your heart, and your actions will be a beacon of light for others to follow."

They gathered their virtual shields, ready to face any challenges that might come their way.

"Our first duty as Digital Heroes is to protect our own digital castle," Maya said. "We'll build strong walls with secure passwords and keep our antivirus shields up to defend against any cyber villains."

"And we'll never let our guard down," Alex added. "We'll stay vigilant and report any suspicious activities to trusted adults. Cybersecurity is a team effort, after all, and we'll never let our guard down!"

Wise Feather nodded, "You have understood well, my young heroes. But remember, being a Digital Hero is not just about protecting yourself. It's also about looking out for others in the digital kingdom."

As they continued their journey, they came across an avatar named KindheartedKai, who had been the victim of cyberbullying in the past.

"We will stand by your side, KindheartedKai," Maya said with determination. "As Digital Heroes, we will support those who need it and stand up against cyberbullying together."

KindheartedKai was touched by their words and felt a newfound sense of empowerment. With the support of Alex, Maya, and the entire virtual community, KindheartedKai was no longer afraid to be true to themselves.

"We will also use our powers to spread kindness and positivity," Alex said. "Our words can have a profound positive impact, and we'll always use them to uplift others and create a welcoming digital kingdom."

As they bid farewell to Wise Feather and prepared to return to the real world, Alex and Maya knew that their adventure had transformed them into Digital Heroes. They understood that being a Digital Hero was not about possessing superpowers but about making responsible choices, standing up for what is right, and using technology for the greater good.

As they returned home, they felt a sense of purpose and determination. They knew that the principles of safe surfing, cybersecurity, kindness, and responsible digital citizenship would guide them not only in the virtual world but also in their daily lives.

And so, their adventure has ended, but their journey as Digital Heroes had just begun. With their capes fluttering in the digital breeze, they were ready to make a positive impact on the digital kingdom and beyond. Armed with their knowledge, compassion, and determination, Alex and Maya were true Digital Heroes, ready to embrace the endless possibilities of the digital world and use their powers to make it a better place for everyone.

Congratulations, Digital Heroes! You've completed "The Internet Adventure" and have gained the superpowers to navigate the digital world safely and responsibly. Remember, the internet is an incredible place filled with exciting possibilities, but it's essential to use it wisely and kindly. By practicing safe surfing, protecting your personal information, and being a Cyberbullying Buster, you can create a positive and happy online space for everyone.

As you continue to explore the digital world, always remember to be a Digital Hero, and spread kindness wherever you go. So, go ahead and enjoy your online adventures, but never forget that with great power comes great responsibility. You are the Digital Heroes of tomorrow, making the internet a safer and happier place for everyone!

Age Group 11-13

"The Digital Pathfinders: Navigating the Online Maze Responsibly"

Chapter 1: Cybersecurity Fundamentals

In the vast and ever-changing digital realm, where magic and technology converge, Cyber Defenders embark on a thrilling quest to protect themselves and others from lurking cyber threats. As Digital Pathfinders, you shall master the art of cybersecurity fundamentals to fortify your digital castles against potential intruders.

Building Strong Passwords
Imagine your digital castle as a magnificent fortress that guards your valuable treasures—your personal information and online accounts. Just like a strong lock protects a treasure chest, a robust password safeguards your digital kingdom from unauthorized access.

To construct a powerful password, you must combine letters (both uppercase and lowercase), numbers, and special characters in a unique sequence. Avoid predictable choices like birthdays or simple words that can be easily guessed by nefarious individuals. Instead, craft a secret code that only you can decipher—a formidable combination that serves as the guardian of your digital treasures.

For instance, rather than using a weak password like "123456" or "password," opt for a mighty passphrase such as "Dragons@Castle42!" This powerful passphrase incorporates complexity, length, and a touch of imagination, making it nearly impervious to malicious attempts.

Remember, Cyber Defenders, your passwords are the keys to your digital realm. Strengthen your defenses with strong passwords to thwart any potential cyber villains seeking to breach your castle walls.

Recognizing Phishing Attempts
In the enchanted landscape of the digital realm, cunning cyber villains may disguise themselves as friendly guides, attempting to deceive you and breach your digital defenses. This malicious art is known as phishing—a deceptive technique where cybercriminals pose as trustworthy entities to trick you into revealing sensitive information or clicking on malicious links.

To outsmart these deceptive beings, you must become astute in recognizing phishing attempts. Watch for suspicious emails, messages, or social media communications that ask for personal information or urge you to click on unknown links. These clever villains may masquerade as familiar entities, such as your school, a social media platform, or an online store.

Be vigilant, young Digital Pathfinders, and always verify the authenticity of any communication before taking any action. If you receive an email requesting personal information or feel uncertain about a message's legitimacy, seek guidance from a trusted adult or authority figure.

Remember, your intuition is a powerful ally in the digital realm. Trust your instincts, and if anything seems amiss, proceed with caution to protect yourself and your fellow Cyber Defenders from the snares of phishing villains.

Protecting Against Online Threats

Beyond the magic of the digital kingdom, unseen dangers lurk in the shadows—malevolent forces like viruses and malware that can infiltrate your digital castle and wreak havoc. As Digital Pathfinders, you must equip yourselves with enchanted shields to defend against these unseen adversaries.

Your magical shields come in the form of reliable antivirus software. These potent tools stand as guardians, scanning your devices for malevolent invaders and neutralizing their harmful intent. Parents regularly update your antivirus shields ensures you have the latest magical charms, safeguarding your kingdom from new and emerging threats.

Embrace the importance of maintaining your digital defenses, for vigilant Cyber Defenders remain ever watchful in their quest to protect their digital domains.

With your knowledge of building strong passwords, recognizing phishing attempts, and protecting against online threats, you are well on your way to becoming formidable Cyber Defenders. Armed with the wisdom of cybersecurity fundamentals, you are now prepared to embark on the next chapter of your digital journey: Ethical Digital Citizenship.

Onward, young Digital Pathfinders, to a realm where knowledge and empathy reign supreme, and responsible digital citizenship guides your way. Through your vigilance and wisdom, the digital realm shall flourish under your watchful eye. May your digital castles stand strong, your passwords remain unbreakable, and your defenses shield against any potential harm. Onward, to Chapter 2: Ethical Digital Citizenship!

Chapter 2: Ethical Digital Citizenship

As the Digital Pathfinders journey through the vast digital kingdom, they realize that their actions hold great power and responsibility. In this chapter, we shall delve deeper into the realm of Ethical Digital Citizenship, where Cyber Defenders learn to navigate with integrity, empathy, and kindness.

Understanding Your Digital Footprint

In the ever-expanding digital realm, every step you take leaves a mark—a trail of information known as your digital footprint. Just as footprints in the sand tell a story, your digital actions paint a picture of who you are in the virtual landscape. As responsible Digital Pathfinders, it is crucial to comprehend the significance of your digital footprint and how it shapes your digital identity and reputation.

Each post, comment, or interaction contributes to the grand tapestry of your online presence. The impressions you make, whether positive or negative, can have far-reaching consequences. Your digital footprint extends beyond the virtual realm, influencing how others perceive you in the physical world as well. You must understand that because you deleted your digital footprint from your sight, does not mean it doesn't still exist in the digital world.

So, young Cyber Defenders, tread carefully and thoughtfully as you leave your digital footprints behind. Be mindful of your actions, and let your digital identity reflect the values you hold dear—integrity, respect, and empathy.

The Power of Responsible Behavior

In the enchanted world of digital interactions, words hold the power to uplift or hurt, to inspire or cause harm. As Digital Pathfinders, you possess the ability to wield this power for good. Embrace the responsibility of using your digital voice to create a positive impact in the virtual community.

Let honesty and integrity be your guide as you navigate the digital landscape. Uphold respectful and ethical behavior, treating others with the same kindness and consideration you would in the physical world. A simple act of compassion, a word of encouragement, or a gesture of support can brighten someone's day and transform the digital realm into a place of harmony.

In the face of adversity or disagreements, remember the Cyber Defender's code of conduct—empathy, respect, and constructive communication. By expressing your opinions with thoughtfulness and empathy, you create an environment where diverse perspectives are valued and understood.

Contributing Positively

In the bustling marketplace of the digital realm, the currency of positivity holds immeasurable value. As Digital Pathfinders, you have the power to make a difference by contributing positively to the virtual community.

Be an agent of inspiration and encouragement, celebrating the achievements of others and supporting their dreams. Embrace a culture of inclusivity, where everyone feels welcomed and valued. By promoting a spirit of collaboration and camaraderie, you nurture a virtual kingdom that thrives on growth and mutual support.

Remember, Cyber Defenders, your positive actions can create a ripple effect, inspiring others to follow your virtuous path. Every act of kindness adds another sparkle to the enchanted world of digital citizenship.

As you journey through the realm of Ethical Digital Citizenship, let the values of integrity, empathy, and kindness guide your every step. Embrace the power of your digital voice and let it resonate with respect and positivity. Together, we shall forge a path towards a digital kingdom where every Cyber Defender thrives in a community of trust and understanding.

Chapter 3: Social Media Smarts

As the Digital Pathfinders venture deeper into the vast digital kingdom, they encounter the vibrant realm of social media—a bustling marketplace where Cyber Defenders connect, share, and communicate. In this chapter, we shall explore the realm of Social Media Smarts, where wisdom and responsibility guide your interactions in this digital landscape.

Navigating Social Media Responsibly

Social media platforms are like bustling towns filled with people from all corners of the digital realm. As you explore this virtual landscape, it is essential to approach your interactions with mindfulness and responsibility.

Before posting, sharing, or commenting, consider the impact your words and images may have on others. Embrace the golden rule of treating others as you wish to be treated. By fostering a culture of respect and empathy, you can create a virtual community that thrives on positivity and constructive dialogue.

Beware of the allure of seeking validation through likes and shares. Instead, focus on meaningful connections and authentic interactions. Your worth is not determined by the number of followers or likes you receive, but by the meaningful connections you build and the positive impact you make in the digital realm.

Setting Privacy Settings

Within the realm of Social Media, magical spells known as privacy settings grant you the power to protect your personal information and control who can see your digital presence. Take the time to understand and customize these settings according to your comfort level.

Limit the information visible to strangers, and allow only trusted friends and family to see more cherished details. By managing your privacy settings, you create a sense of security within your virtual kingdom, ensuring that only those you trust can peer into your digital castle.

Remember, your privacy is a precious treasure, and as Cyber Defenders, you must protect it with diligence and care.

Avoiding Oversharing

In the digital realm, it is essential to remember that not every aspect of your life needs to be on public display. Beware of oversharing personal details, such as your exact location, contact information, or daily routines.

As Digital Pathfinders, you must be cautious guardians of your virtual selves, knowing when to share and when to keep certain aspects of your lives private. By striking this delicate balance, you maintain a sense of control over your digital identity and protect yourself from potential risks.

Embrace the magic of being selective in what you share, focusing on meaningful and positive interactions that contribute to the digital community in a meaningful way.

As you navigate the world of Social Media, remember that your actions have consequences and can impact the lives of others. Embrace the values of respect, kindness, and empathy in all your digital interactions. By doing so, you shall build bridges of understanding and friendship, transforming the digital realm into a place of harmony and growth.

Onward, young Digital Pathfinders, let the magic of responsible social media usage guide your way, and may your digital presence be a beacon of positivity in the vast digital kingdom. May you wield the power of empathy and mindfulness to create a virtual realm where every Cyber Defender thrives and flourishes.

Chapter 4: Cyberbullying Prevention

As the Digital Pathfinders delve further into the enchanted digital kingdom, they encounter the shadows of cyberbullying—a dark cloud that casts a shadow over the digital landscape. In this chapter, we shall explore the realm of Cyberbullying Prevention, where Cyber Defenders learn to recognize, prevent, and combat this insidious threat.

Recognizing Cyberbullying

Just as a vigilant watchman guards the kingdom, you, as Cyber Defenders, must remain vigilant against the signs of cyberbullying. Cyberbullying takes various forms in the digital realm, such as hurtful comments, spreading rumors, sharing embarrassing photos, or excluding others from online groups.

To combat this malevolent force, you must sharpen your perception and develop empathy. Be aware of sudden changes in someone's behavior, unexplained sadness, or withdrawal from online activities. These may be signs that someone is silently suffering from the effects of cyberbullying.

As Digital Pathfinders, you must be empathetic protectors, standing united against cyberbullying and offering support to those in need.

Strategies to Prevent Cyberbullying

As Cyber Defenders, your mission is not just to identify cyberbullying but to prevent it from taking root. The power to create a virtual kingdom free from cyberbullying lies in your actions and choices.

Encourage open communication with friends, family, and teachers, so everyone feels comfortable seeking help when needed. Establish a culture of respect and empathy, where cyberbullying is not tolerated, and kindness prevails.

Be the beacon of positivity and encourage your peers to treat others with empathy and understanding. Together, let us cultivate an atmosphere where differences are celebrated, and every voice is valued.

Reporting and Seeking Help

In the digital realm, standing against cyberbullying requires collective action. If you encounter cyberbullying or witness it happening to someone else, take immediate steps to report the incident.

Most social media platforms and online communities have reporting mechanisms to notify the administrators of harmful content or behavior. By reporting cyberbullying, you can play a crucial role in curbing its spread and protecting potential victims.

Furthermore, never hesitate to seek help from trusted adults or authorities. Cyberbullying should never be faced alone. Reach out to parents, teachers, or school counselors, who can provide guidance and support during difficult times.

Remember, Cyber Defenders, you are not alone in this battle. By working together, we can create a virtual kingdom where empathy and respect flourish, and cyberbullying finds no place to thrive.

Cultivating Digital Empathy

In the realm of Cyber Defenders, empathy becomes a potent shield against cyberbullying. As you interact with others online, remember the importance of empathy—the ability to understand and share the feelings of others.

Choose your digital words with care, for they have the power to heal or harm. Avoid engaging in hurtful behavior, and be a positive force in the digital community. Reach out to those who may be struggling, offering a listening ear and a helping hand.

By cultivating digital empathy, you create a safe haven within the digital realm, where every Cyber Defender feels seen, heard, and valued.

Together, we shall stand firm against cyberbullying, replacing darkness with the brilliance of understanding and unity. In our digital journey, may your digital interactions inspire a realm where kindness prevails, and every Cyber Defender thrives in a world free from cyberbullying.

Chapter 5: Online Relationships & avoiding Catfishing.

As the Digital Pathfinders continue their quest through the enchanting digital kingdom, they encounter the realm of Online Relationships—a place where connections are formed, and friendships are forged through the magic of technology. In this chapter, we shall explore the intricacies of Online Relationships and understand the risks and challenges that come with building connections in this virtual landscape.

The World of Online Friendships

Within the vast digital realm, you may encounter avatars from different corners of the world, each with unique stories and interests. Online friendships can be an enriching experience, as you connect with individuals who share your passions and dreams. However, it is vital to approach these relationships with discernment and caution.

As Cyber Defenders, you must be wise navigators, acknowledging the potential for genuine connections while also being aware of hidden intentions. Not everyone you meet in the digital realm may have your best interests at heart, so it is essential to proceed with mindfulness.

Safeguarding Your Boundaries

While forming online friendships can be exciting, safeguarding your boundaries is of utmost importance. Protect your personal information and share it sparingly, ensuring that you do not disclose sensitive details such as your family, home address, phone number, or financial information.

As Digital Pathfinders, you must be vigilant guardians of your privacy. Only reveal information to individuals you trust and those who have earned the privilege of being part of your inner circle. By doing so, you maintain a sense of control over your digital kingdom, keeping it safe from potential risks.

Navigating Tricky Situations

In the realm of Online Relationships, you may encounter tricky situations that challenge your judgment and emotions. Beware of individuals who may try to manipulate or exploit your trust. Be cautious of sharing personal feelings or engaging in intimate conversations with strangers, as they may have ulterior motives.

If something feels uncomfortable or suspicious, trust your instincts and seek guidance from trusted adults. Remember, Cyber Defenders, your well-being is of the utmost importance, and you have the right to prioritize your safety and emotional well-being.

The Quest for Authenticity

In the realm of Online Relationships, authenticity is a precious treasure. Strive to be your true self and encourage others to do the same. Honesty and transparency create an atmosphere of trust and genuine connection.

Be cautious of individuals who may create false personas or pretend to be someone they are not to catfish you and lure you into sharing personal information. As Cyber Defenders, you must value authenticity and foster an environment where honesty is celebrated and cherished.

Handling Online Conflict

In the digital landscape, conflicts may arise, just as they do in the physical world. When facing disagreements, approach them with empathy and open communication. Seek to understand the perspectives of others and find common ground. Understand, that when not everyone shares the same point of view, and it is important to agree to disagree agreeably about any subject.

As Cyber Defenders, you aim to resolve conflicts peacefully, nurturing an environment of mutual respect. Avoid engaging in cyberbullying or retaliatory behavior, for kindness and empathy are the true weapons of diplomacy in the virtual realm.

The Value of Offline Connections

While Online Relationships can be meaningful and enriching, remember the importance of balancing virtual connections with real-world experiences. Spend time with friends and family offline, engage in activities that foster genuine bonds, and nurture your real-world relationships. It is easier to see the true character of someone in person rather than online.

These offline connections are the bedrock of support and understanding, offering a sense of stability, and belonging that complements your virtual experiences.

As you navigate the realm of Online Relationships, let good judgement and authenticity guide your interactions. Cherish the connections that bring positivity and growth to your digital kingdom, and approach each new relationship with a blend of caution and an open heart.

Chapter 6: Becoming a Cyber Defender

As the Digital Pathfinders journey deeper into the enchanting digital kingdom, they embrace the mantle of Cyber Defenders—a noble title bestowed upon those who safeguard the virtual realm with wisdom and courage. In this chapter, we shall delve into the realm of Becoming a Cyber Defender, where critical thinking skills and responsible digital citizenship pave the way for a safer and thriving digital landscape.

Critical Thinking Online

Using critical thinking to discern fact from fiction, Cyber Defenders must navigate the ever-evolving digital realm where information flows like a mighty river, carrying both truths and falsehoods.

Question the source, credibility, and intention behind every piece of information encountered online. Don't accept information at face value; instead, verify facts from reliable sources and consult experts when needed.

Critical thinking is your most potent weapon against misinformation and manipulation. By honing this skill, you shall navigate the digital maze with clarity and confidence.

Evaluating Online Information

Within the vast digital kingdom, not all that glitters is gold. Beware of misinformation and misleading content that may try to deceive and mislead. As Cyber Defenders, you must be savvy information seekers, adept at evaluating the credibility of online sources.

Consider multiple perspectives and cross-reference information from reputable sources before accepting it as accurate. Separate opinions from facts and be cautious of sensational headlines or clickbait that seeks to manipulate your emotions.

You may now rise as protectors of truth in the digital realm.

Staying Safe on the Internet

As Cyber Defenders, your safety and well-being are paramount. Protect your digital castle with the knowledge acquired throughout your quest.

Use strong passwords, keep your software up to dated, and remain cautious when sharing personal information. Be wary of phishing attempts and suspicious links that may seek to infiltrate your digital defenses.

Regularly review your privacy settings on social media platforms and other online services, ensuring that you have control over what information is visible to others.

By staying vigilant, you safeguard yourself and others from potential threats, keeping the digital realm secure for all Cyber Defenders. Ensure you identify red flags, such as sites asking for your personal information, emails that look too good to be true, social media sites that have sent emails with links or asking for you to log into your account.

Embracing Lifelong Learning

In the ever-changing digital kingdom, learning is an ongoing adventure. As Cyber Defenders, embrace the joy of discovery and curiosity. Continuously educate yourself on new technologies, online trends, and digital safety practices.

Stay informed about the latest cybersecurity practices and threats, as well as the evolving landscape of digital ethics. As you expand your knowledge, you position yourself at the forefront of digital guardianship.

Never cease to explore and learn, for knowledge empowers you to make informed decisions and lead by example.

Leading by Example

As Digital Pathfinders, you have learned the essence of ethical behavior and responsible digital citizenship. Now, as Cyber Defenders, you shall lead by example, inspiring others to follow your virtuous path.

Be the guiding light of empathy, kindness, and integrity in the digital realm. Use your voice to promote positive interactions, combat cyberbullying, and stand up against online negativity.

Through your actions, you shall inspire a new generation of responsible digital citizens who contribute positively to the digital community.

Making a Difference

Armed with critical thinking and a strong moral compass, you have the power to make a difference in the digital kingdom. Stand against cyberbullying, promote kindness, and protect the vulnerable.

Use your digital voice to amplify important causes, share positive messages, and contribute to a virtual realm where empathy and understanding prevail.

By being proactive Cyber Defenders, you create a ripple effect of positive change, fostering a virtual world that reflects the values of respect, empathy, and digital courage.

The Journey Continues

As we conclude this chapter and your quest as Digital Pathfinders, remember that the journey as a Cyber Defender is never truly over.

The digital realm will continue to evolve, presenting new challenges and opportunities. As Digital Pathfinders, you shall forever be Cyber Defenders, protectors of the digital kingdom, and champions of responsible and ethical digital citizenship.

Remember, the digital realm is filled with endless opportunities, but it is up to you to use technology wisely and spread positivity in every virtual corner.

With your hearts filled with wisdom, courage, and compassion, venture forth as ambassadors of positive change. As the guardians of the digital realm, you are now ready to shape the future of the digital landscape for the better.

Onward, young Cyber Defenders, to a world were empathy and critical thinking reign supreme. You have successfully navigated the online maze and become Cyber Defenders, armed with knowledge, empathy, and the power of responsible digital citizenship.

As you continue your digital journey, may you be a shining example of ethical behavior, empathy, and digital courage.

Age Group 14-17

"Guardians of the Digital Realm: Empowering Responsible Online Citizenship"

Chapter 1: Digital Footprint and Reputation Management

As guardians of the digital realm, all Cyber Defenders must be conscious of the lasting imprints they leave in the digital landscape. In this chapter, we shall explore the significance of your digital footprint and reputation, and how to cultivate a positive digital identity.

Understanding Your Digital Footprint

Your digital footprint is like a tapestry that weaves together every online action you take. From social media posts and comments to website interactions and online purchases, each step leaves a mark that shapes your digital identity.

As Cyber Defenders, understanding your digital footprint is crucial. Every piece of information you share, or post can be seen, analyzed, and sometimes even preserved by others. Your digital footprint reveals insights into your personality, interests, and activities. It can influence how others perceive you and impact opportunities such as college admissions, job interviews, and personal relationships.

Take a moment to explore your digital footprint by searching for your name online. Examine the content that is associated with your digital identity, and consider whether it reflects the person you want to be. By being mindful of your online actions, you can shape your digital footprint and craft a positive and authentic digital identity.

Maintaining a Positive Digital Identity

Your digital identity is a reflection of your character and values. Nurturing a positive digital reputation is essential for establishing trust and credibility in the virtual realm.

To maintain a positive digital identity:

Be Authentic: Share your passions, accomplishments, and experiences genuinely. Embrace your uniqueness and let your digital persona align with your real-life self.

Engage Positively: Interact with others in a respectful and constructive manner. Avoid engaging in online conflicts or participating in harmful activities.

Curate Your Content: Be mindful of the content you create and share. Consider how it may impact others and the reputation you want to build. Once your content is posted, it can be copied without your knowledge or permission and shared.

Seek Growth: Embrace opportunities for personal growth and learning. Share your interests and achievements with humility and enthusiasm.

Stay Informed: Be aware of the latest privacy settings and security measures on social media platforms. Regularly review and adjust your settings to control what others can see.

Learn from Mistakes: If you make a mistake online, take responsibility for it and learn from the experience. Apologize if necessary and strive to do better in the future.

By taking deliberate steps to cultivate a positive digital identity, you shall become a trusted and respected presence in the digital realm. Remember, your digital identity is an extension of your character, and as Cyber Defenders, your actions shall speak volumes about the integrity you uphold.

As we continue our quest to become responsible Digital Citizens, let us carry these principles in our hearts and minds, empowering ourselves and others to navigate the digital landscape with wisdom and grace. Onward, young Cyber Defenders, to Chapter 3: Cyber Ethics!

Chapter 2: Social Media Influence

In the enchanting realm of social media, young Cyber Defenders must be wise navigators, aware of the impact it has on their mental health and well-being. In this chapter, we shall explore the influence of social media and the importance of developing healthy online habits.

Recognizing Social Media's Impact

Social media platforms hold the power to connect people from around the world, providing a platform for sharing experiences, ideas, and creativity. However, the virtual landscape of social media can also exert significant influence on your mental health and self-perception.

Understanding the impact of social media on your well-being is vital. Constant comparison to others, the pursuit of validation through likes and comments, and exposure to unrealistic standards can all affect your mental health and self-esteem. Recognize the potential pitfalls and challenges of social media and develop strategies to protect your well-being.

Developing Healthy Online Habits

To navigate the realm of social media responsibly, Cyber Defenders must cultivate healthy online habits and mindful engagement that prioritize well-being and digital balance.

1. Mindful Engagement: Be mindful of your social media usage and the emotions it evokes. If you find yourself feeling overwhelmed or negative, take breaks from social media and engage in activities that promote relaxation and self-care.

2. Quality over Quantity: Focus on cultivating meaningful connections and interactions on social media rather than seeking validation through numbers. The value of your digital presence lies not in the quantity of followers but in the quality of your engagements.

3. Curate Your Feed: Choose to follow accounts that inspire and uplift you. Curate your social media feed to promote positivity, diversity, and creativity.

4. **Balance Online and Offline Life:** Strike a healthy balance between your online and offline activities. Engage in hobbies, sports or read a book, and spending time with loved ones outside the digital realm.

5. **Digital Empathy:** Be kind and supportive to others on social media. Avoid participating in online conflicts or spreading negativity. Empathy is a powerful force that can contribute to a positive virtual community.

By developing healthy online habits, you can harness the potential of social media for positive connections and personal growth. Remember, social media is a tool that you wield, you shall use it with wisdom and intention.

Digital Respect: Protecting your Online Persona

In the age of smartphones and social media, teenagers like you have the power to connect, share, and express yourselves like never before. But with great power comes great responsibility, and it's crucial to understand how to navigate the digital world with respect and caution.

As you embark on this journey, imagine you're in a virtual classroom where a knowledgeable mentor is about to guide you through the importance of not sharing explicit pictures with partners or posting them online.

Today, we're going to talk about something very important – protecting your online persona. In this digital age, where sharing moments and emotions is so easy, it's vital to be mindful of the content you share and its potential consequences through the importance of not sharing explicit pictures with partners or posting them online.

Imagine you're sitting in front of your computer or holding your phone. You might be tempted or coerced to send a revealing picture to your boyfriend or girlfriend – someone you trust. But before you hit that send button, pause, and consider a few things...

1. **Digital Footprint:** When you share a picture online, it's like leaving a footprint in the sand – it doesn't easily wash away. Even if you trust the person, you're sending it to, there's always a risk of the picture getting into the wrong hands.

2. **Trust and Consent:** Trust is essential in any relationship, but it's important to remember that trust can be broken, unintentionally or otherwise. With Apps or controls on everyone's phones, screen recording or capture features are very possible. Also, just because you're in a relationship doesn't mean you've given blanket consent for explicit content to be shared.

3. **Privacy Settings Aren't Foolproof:** You might think that setting your social media accounts to "private" will keep your pictures safe. But even private accounts can be hacked or manipulated. And once something is online, there is no control over who sees it.

4. **The Ripple Effect:** Imagine if the picture you sent ends up being shared without your consent. It could spread like wildfire, and you might find yourself facing embarrassment, humiliation, or even bullying. Once it's out there, it's tough to take back.

5. **Long-Term Consequences:** As you grow and mature, your perspective on what you shared might change. You might regret the decisions you made when you were younger. Those pictures could

come back to haunt you in unexpected ways, affecting college applications, job searches, and more.

Remember, the digital world can be a wonderful place to express yourself and connect with others, but it's also a place where things can go wrong quickly. Before you share explicit content, take a step back and ask yourself if it's worth the potential risks.

If someone is pressuring you to share explicit content against your will, it's important to remember that this is not a healthy or respectful relationship. Respect and consent should always be at the forefront of any interaction, both online and offline.

You have the power to shape your digital footprint and create a positive online presence. By treating yourselves and others with respect and understanding the potential consequences of your actions, you're taking the first step toward becoming responsible digital citizens.

So, think twice before sharing your content, and to prioritize respect, trust, and consent in all of our digital interactions. Remember, you have the power to shape your digital world – make it a world you're proud to be a part of.

As we continue our quest to become responsible Digital Citizens, let us navigate the realm of social media with resilience and digital balance. The power to shape the influence of social media lies within each of us, and through our actions, we shall create a virtual kingdom that nurtures mental well-being and promotes positivity.

Chapter 3: Cyber Ethics

In the vast digital kingdom, the code of Cyber Ethics guides the actions and behaviors of responsible Cyber Defenders. In this chapter, we shall explore the ethical considerations of technology use and the importance of respecting others' rights online.

Exploring Cyber Ethics

Cyber Ethics is the moral compass that steers your behavior in the digital realm. It encompasses a set of principles and values that govern how you interact with technology, data, and others online. As Cyber Defenders, understanding Cyber Ethics is paramount to fostering a safe and respectful digital community.

Consider the following ethical considerations:

Privacy: Respect the privacy of others by not sharing their personal information without consent. Be mindful of the information you share and consider the potential impact on others.

Digital Ownership: Respect the intellectual property of others, including copyrighted materials, and give proper credit when using or sharing content created by others.

Honesty and Integrity: Be truthful and honest in your online interactions. Avoid spreading misinformation or participating in deceptive practices.

Digital Empathy: Treat others with empathy and kindness, just as you would in face-to-face interactions. Consider the feelings and perspectives of others before engaging in online discussions.

Cybersecurity Awareness: Use technology responsibly and be aware of cybersecurity best practices to protect yourself and others from potential threats.

Respecting Others' Rights Online

In the interconnected digital realm, the rights of others must be respected with the same fervor as your own. As Cyber Defenders, you shall become the champions of digital rights and online civility.

Freedom of Expression: Respect the right of others to express their opinions and ideas, even if they differ from your own. Engage in healthy debates and discussions without resorting to personal attacks.

Digital Inclusivity: Promote a culture of inclusivity where diverse perspectives and voices are welcome and valued. Avoid engaging in discriminatory behavior or hate speech.

Cyberbullying Prevention: Take a stand against cyberbullying and support those who may be affected. Report instances of cyberbullying and encourage others to do the same.

Digital Empowerment: Use technology to empower others and make a positive impact. Support initiatives that aim to bridge the digital divide and ensure equal access to technology and information.

Responsible Content Sharing: Be cautious about sharing content that may be harmful, offensive, or misleading. Verify the accuracy and credibility of information before disseminating it.

By upholding the principles of Cyber Ethics and respecting others' rights online, you shall create a virtual kingdom where mutual respect and understanding thrive. Remember, your digital actions shape the culture of the digital realm, and as Cyber Defenders, you have the power to foster a positive and compassionate online community.

As we venture onward in our quest to become responsible Digital Citizens, let us carry the torch of Cyber Ethics with unwavering dedication. The digital kingdom awaits our leadership, and through our actions, we shall create a realm of integrity and respect. Onward, young Cyber Defenders, to Chapter 4: Social Media Influence!

Chapter 4: Cyberbullying Intervention

In the digital kingdom, where connections are made through the magic of technology, Cyber Defenders aged 14-17 must stand united against the shadows of cyberbullying. In this chapter, we shall explore the importance of taking action against cyberbullying and supporting others who may be affected.

Taking Action Against Cyberbullying

Cyberbullying is a dark cloud that casts a shadow over the digital realm, inflicting emotional harm on its victims. As Cyber Defenders, it is our duty to be the rays of light that break through this darkness. Recognize the signs of cyberbullying, which can include hurtful comments, threats, rumors, or the exclusion of others from online groups.

If you witness cyberbullying, take action:

Speak Up: Stand up against cyberbullying and advocate for a culture of kindness and respect online. Encourage others to do the same.

Report Incidents: Report cyberbullying incidents to the appropriate authorities on the platform where it occurred. This helps ensure the safety of the digital community.

Offer Support: Reach out to the victim privately and offer your support. A kind word or gesture can make a significant difference to someone who may be suffering.

Involve Trusted Adults: If the cyberbullying involves serious threats or harassment, involve trusted adults such as parents, teachers, or school counselors. They can provide additional support and intervention if needed.

Promote Positive Digital Citizenship: Encourage others to be responsible Digital Citizens, treating others with empathy and respect in the digital realm.

Supporting Others

Empathy is our guiding compass. Be attentive to those who may be affected by cyberbullying, offering a listening ear and a comforting presence. Cyberbullying can be isolating, and your support can make a world of difference to someone who feels alone.

Validate Their Feelings: Let the victim know that their feelings are valid and that they are not alone in their experience.

Encourage Open Communication: Encourage the victim to talk about their feelings and experiences. Offer a safe space for them to express themselves.

Stand in Solidarity: Show solidarity with the victim by offering your support publicly or privately. Sometimes, knowing that others care can provide immense comfort.

Help Seek Assistance: If the situation escalates or becomes overwhelming, encourage the victim to seek help from trusted adults or professionals.

Promote Digital Kindness: Spread the message of digital kindness and encourage others to be compassionate and respectful in their online interactions.

By taking action against cyberbullying and supporting those who may be affected, you become a defender of the digital realm, shielding others from harm, and spreading compassion and empathy throughout the virtual kingdom.

As we continue our quest to become responsible Digital Citizens, let us remember the power of our actions in creating a supportive and kind digital community. Together, as Cyber Defenders, we shall stand tall against cyberbullying and promote a realm of digital harmony. Onward, young Cyber Defenders, to Chapter 6: Cybersecurity Careers!

Chapter 5: Cybersecurity Careers

In the digital realm, where the magic of technology intertwines with the responsibility of protecting the virtual kingdom, Cyber Defenders aged 14-17 shall explore the realm of Cybersecurity Careers. In this chapter, we shall embark on a journey to understand various careers in cybersecurity and the significance of skilled professionals in safeguarding the digital world.

Exploring Careers in Cybersecurity

The realm of cybersecurity offers a plethora of exciting and diverse career paths for aspiring Cyber Defenders. As technology evolves, so do the challenges of securing the digital landscape, making skilled cybersecurity professionals essential guardians of the virtual realm.

Explore various careers in cybersecurity:

1. Ethical Hacker: These virtuous hackers use their skills to identify vulnerabilities in systems and networks, helping organizations strengthen their defenses.

2. Cybersecurity Analyst: Analysts monitor networks for suspicious activity and respond to cyber threats, safeguarding sensitive information.

3. Digital Forensics Investigator: These detectives unravel cybercrimes, collecting and analyzing digital evidence to catch cyber villains.

4. Information Security Manager: Managers oversee the implementation of security measures and ensure organizations comply with cybersecurity regulations.

5. Penetration Tester: Testers simulate cyberattacks to assess an organization's vulnerabilities and devise strategies to fortify defenses.

6. Security Consultant: Consultants advise organizations on cybersecurity best practices, helping them develop robust security strategies.

The Importance of Skilled Professionals

As Cyber Defenders, you are the future guardians of the digital kingdom. Skilled cybersecurity professionals are the pillars that support the digital realm, defending against cyber threats and ensuring the safety of online systems.

Understand the significance of cybersecurity professionals:

1. Protecting Personal Data: Cybersecurity professionals play a vital role in safeguarding personal information, preventing data breaches, and protecting individuals from identity theft.

2. Safeguarding Organizations: Cyberattacks can disrupt businesses and compromise sensitive information. Skilled professionals fortify defenses, preventing financial losses and maintaining trust with customers.

3. National Security: Cybersecurity is crucial for national defense, as cyber threats can target critical infrastructure and government systems.

4. Fostering Digital Innovation: By providing a secure environment, cybersecurity professionals enable technological advancements and digital innovation to flourish.

5. Promoting Responsible Digital Citizenship: Skilled professionals raise awareness of cybersecurity best practices, empowering individuals to be responsible Digital Citizens.

As you explore careers in cybersecurity, consider your passions, strengths, and interests. Your journey as Cyber Defenders can lead you to become the guardians of digital safety and pioneers of the future digital landscape.

With determination and a commitment to lifelong learning, you shall emerge as the skilled Cyber Defenders that the digital realm needs. Onward, young Cyber Defenders, to a future where the virtual kingdom thrives under your expert guardianship!

Chapter 6: Advanced Cybersecurity

As the guardians of the digital realm, Cyber Defenders must strengthen their defenses to protect themselves and others from the ever-evolving threats in the digital landscape. In this chapter, we shall embark on a journey through Advanced Cybersecurity, where you will delve into the realm of encryption, secure Wi-Fi usage, and safeguarding personal data.

The Power of Encryption

Encryption is a digital veil that transforms your digital messages and data into unreadable code. Imagine it as a secret language known only to you and the intended recipient. As Cyber Defenders, understanding encryption is vital to safeguard your communications from prying eyes.

Encryption works like a lock and key: your message is the treasure you want to keep safe, and the encryption algorithm is the lock that scrambles the treasure. Only the recipient with the correct key can unlock and decipher the message. By mastering encryption techniques, you gain the ability to communicate securely, shield sensitive information, and protect yourself from cyber attackers seeking to intercept your digital treasures.

From private messages to financial transactions, encryption acts as your shield against potential cyber villains, ensuring that your most valuable digital possessions remain safe from harm.

Navigating Secure Wi-Fi Usage

Wi-Fi networks are like bridges that connect you to the vast digital realm, allowing you to access information, communicate, and explore. However, not all Wi-Fi bridges are safe to cross. Unsecured Wi-Fi networks in public places, such as cafes or airports, can be vulnerable to cybercriminals who may intercept your data.

As Cyber Defenders, you must become skilled navigators, distinguishing secure Wi-Fi networks from unsecured ones. Secure networks require a password for access and provide encryption, protecting your data from unauthorized eavesdroppers. Conversely, unsecured networks lack these protections, leaving your digital castle vulnerable to potential attacks.

To navigate the Wi-Fi landscape safely, connect only to secure networks whenever possible. When using public Wi-Fi, exercise caution when accessing sensitive information, such as banking or personal accounts. Consider using a Virtual Private Network (VPN) to add an extra layer of protection, ensuring your data remains shielded from potential cyber threats.

Protecting Personal Data

In the digital realm, personal data is a treasure sought after by cyber villains. From your name and address to financial information and browsing habits, these digital gems provide insights into your life and interests.

As Cyber Defenders, you shall become the guardians of your personal data, understanding its value and how to protect it from falling into the wrong hands. Be cautious when sharing personal information online, and refrain from divulging unnecessary details. Regularly review your privacy settings on social media platforms and other online accounts to control who can access your information.

Phishing is another technique used by cybercriminals to trick individuals into revealing sensitive information. Be wary of unsolicited emails or messages requesting personal data, and never click on suspicious links or download attachments from unknown sources.

By safeguarding your personal data, you build a digital fortress that thwarts cyber villains and ensures your digital identity remains intact. Remember, the power to protect your digital kingdom lies in your hands, and by mastering the art of Advanced Cybersecurity, you become the formidable Cyber Defender that the digital realm needs.

Made in the USA
Columbia, SC
14 October 2023